Exploring the World Below

by Kathy Furgang

MW01109097

Scott Foresman
is an imprint of

PEARSON

Glenview, Illinois • Boston, Massachusetts • Chandler, Arizona •
Upper Saddle River, New Jersey

Photographs

Every effort has been made to secure permission and provide appropriate credit for photographic material. The publisher deeply regrets any omission and pledges to correct errors called to its attention in subsequent editions.

Unless otherwise acknowledged, all photographs are the property of Pearson Education, Inc.

Photo locators denoted as follows: Top (T), Center (C), Bottom (B), Left (L), Right (R), Background (Bkgd)

Opener Emory Kristof and Alvin Chandler/National Geographic Image Collection; **1** Norbert Wu/Minden Pictures/National Geographic Image Collection; **3** ©UpperCut Images/SuperStock; **4** Art Resource, NY; **5** Bettman/Corbis; **6** Bettman/Corbis; **7** Bettman/Corbis, Bettmann/Corbis; **9** Julian Patridge/Nature Picture Library; **10** NOAA; **12** Norbert Wu/Minden Pictures/National Geographic Image Collection; **14** Emory Kristof and Alvin Chandler/National Geographic Image Collection; **15** NGS Image Collection/National Geographic Image Collection; **16** David McLain/Aurora/Getty Images; **18** (TL) Roger Viollet/Getty Images, (TR) Time Life Pictures/US Navy/Time Life Pictures/Getty Images; **19** (TL) Bates Littlehales/National Geographic Image Collection, (TR) Tim MacMillan/©AP Images; **20** (TR) Central Press/Hulton Archive/Getty Images, (CL) Georges Houot, (CR) NOAA, (TL) Ralph White/Corbis; **21** (TR) ©Woods Hole Oceanographic Institution, (CR, CL) NOAA, (TL) Ralph White/Corbis.

ISBN 13: 978-0-328-52622-2
ISBN 10:   0-328-52622-3

3 4 5 6 7 V0N4 17 16 15 14 13 12 11 10

Despite our best attempts to explore it, the ocean still seems limitless.

Exploring the Deep Blue Sea

Have you ever been on a ship looking out over the ocean and wondered what was in that deep blue sea? The ocean covers nearly three-quarters of Earth's surface, but most of it still remains unexplored. Some areas of the ocean are as deep as a mountain is tall!

Humans have wondered and dreamed about the ocean for thousands of years. Our imaginations make us curious about hidden worlds. What is the deep ocean like? What lives there, and how does it survive? Until the past century, many of those questions went unanswered. Now, because of new technology, we are learning more every day about the depths of the ocean and its peculiar animal inhabitants—from shrimp to sharks, from sea jellies to sponges.

Submersibles have come a long way since Alexander the Great's barrel.

Early Starts

Explorers are **intrepid** by nature. They endure harsh climates and other dangers in order to visit almost every place on Earth's surface. But how can people explore where there is no air to breathe, and worse, crushing pressure weighing down on all sides? That's why the ocean's depths remain largely hidden from us even today.

For centuries, people explored the ocean by ship. But they were not able to journey very far below its surface. One of the first known attempts to peek under the surface of the sea may have happened around 333 BCE. According to legend, Alexander the Great was lowered into the Aegean Sea in a barrel-shaped glass container. The container allowed him to breathe, stay dry, and reach areas that swimmers could not. He reported seeing strange underwater animals that had never been seen before.

The Diving Bell

In the 1400s and 1500s, grand wooden ships began to travel across oceans. When people saw how vast the oceans were, they became even more interested in what was below the surface—especially as treasure-laden ships sank and were lost forever.

The diving bell gave the world its first extended look at life beneath the sea.

In 1531 Italian inventor Guglielmo de Lorena designed a device that allowed people to explore sunken ships at the bottom of a lake. The diving bell was small and just fit around the diver's upper body. Divers could use the device to stay underwater for only a short time because it did not hold much air for them to breathe. It can be considered to be one of the first submarines.

People eventually improved on the design of the diving bell. Some versions had larger air tanks and tubes for breathing. Some had room for several divers to fit inside, with tubes leading to the surface to provide air. Soon sea explorers were as fascinated by the spectacular variety of life beneath the waves as they were about the treasures that had been lost in shipwrecks.

A. Engine-Room.—C. Smoke-Stack.—D. Munition-Room.—E. Coal-Bunkers.—F. Look-Out.—I. 1, 1. Compartments for Air or Water.—0, 0, 0. Compartments for Compressed Air

LONGITUDINAL SECTION OF SUBMARINE BATTERY.

Would you go underwater in something that looks like this?

How Low Can You Go?

In the 1600s, the first true submarine was invented. It carried a crew of people and traveled under the ocean's surface as well as floating on top of it. Over the years and centuries that followed, subs became reliable enough for both transportation and warfare. Today's submarines can be as small as a car or as large as two jumbo-jets. Some submarines are designed for short trips, while others can go around the world without refueling. But they are rarely used for exploring the ocean bottom.

Ocean explorers wanted a device that could go into the deeper parts of the ocean, far from shore. For many years, most submarines went only a few hundred feet below the surface of the ocean. This is because the water pressure at lower depths is greater than the submarines could bear.

The weight of water puts pressure on any object in the ocean. The deeper an object is in the ocean, the more water pressure the object has to withstand. Going

The first bathysphere was invented by William Beebe and Otis Barton in 1930 and tested in 1934.

The bathyscaphe *FNRS 3* dived 13,287 feet below the ocean's surface in 1954.

one hundred feet below the surface puts almost sixty pounds of pressure on an object. At greater depths, early submarines would have cracked, sprung leaks, or simply collapsed.

In 1930 two scientists created an underwater chamber called a bathysphere that could travel 1,428 feet (435.3 meters) below the surface. It had thick steel walls and could stand up against tons of water pressure. Its crew kept breaking their own record by continuing to explore areas farther below the surface. With each journey, they saw amazing animals living in areas where people thought none would be able to survive.

The first vehicles to travel far below the surface were called **submersibles**. They were very small and allowed for only a person or two to fit inside. Throughout the early part of the 1900s, each new submersible vehicle inspired other explorers to explore even deeper. By 1954 a bathyscaphe or "deep boat" named *FNRS 3* had traveled 13,287 feet, or more than two miles, below the surface. It's hard to imagine, but with each mile farther down, an additional ton of water pressure pressed on the vehicle!

By the 1960s and 1970s, submersibles were reaching even greater depths. Many of these undersea vehicles were launched from ships in the middle of the ocean. Battery-powered thrusters provided **propulsion** that enabled the subs to move forward and be steered.

The new submersibles had a small compartment for the divers and a glass window for viewing the underwater world around the vessel. The air inside was kept at a comfortable pressure that allowed crew members to move freely, and a tightly sealed **hatch** kept the crushing weight of the water safely outside.

Scientists in some submersibles could even use robotic arms to collect samples of ocean plants or animals to be studied in a laboratory back on the surface.

Oceanographers who took submersibles to new depths in the 1960s and 1970s had little room, but they did get a great view of the ocean.

9

ROVs: Greater Depth

Despite improvements in the design of submersibles, the water pressure miles below the ocean's surface still makes parts of the deep sea too difficult and dangerous for humans to explore. Just as robots have been sent to Mars to collect information and take pictures, many submersibles that travel to the cold, dark depths of the ocean are robots.

One type of underwater robot is known as a Remotely Operated Vehicle, or ROV. It may be sent down into the ocean while being operated by humans from the safety of a ship on the surface. ROVs have cameras that photograph new areas and devices that collect samples from the ocean floor. Some ROVs do repairs on offshore oil-drilling platforms and undersea pipelines.

The advantage of having a robot do such jobs is that it keeps humans out of harm's way. Every time a person goes to these depths, they are exposed to the dangers of enormous pressure, possible collisions with underwater objects, loss of contact with the surface, and structural failure. ROVs make all these risks unnecessary.

Some ROVs and other submersibles remain closer to the surface of the water, connected to a submarine by

A Remotely Operated Vehicle gets to parts of the ocean floor humans can't reach.

means of a long cable that prevents them getting lost or shipwrecked during their explorations. The connection to the submarine also provides power to the submersible, along with oxygen when there are humans aboard.

Crews sometimes operate these remote-controlled submersibles from the submarines, rather than from a research station on the ocean's surface. This means that the ROV may be used anywhere on the globe as needed. Such "tethered" ROVs allow a submarine crew to examine their underwater environment or even to inspect the outer shell of their own submerged vessel.

Mysteries of the Deep

What kinds of amazing discoveries have submersibles made? What kinds of questions do they answer for scientists? Is the deep ocean bottom sandy, covered in **silt**, as the floor of a lake? Or is it solid rock? How deep is the ocean?

Submersible crews try to find as many answers as they can. They have brought back pictures of volcanic vents on the ocean floor that have shown how mountains form on

A rare look at deep-sea fish species makes undersea travel worthwhile.

the bottom of the sea, completely hidden from sight. Before those pictures were taken, no one even knew what the ocean bottom looked like!

Astonishing underwater animals can also be seen through submersible cameras. A submersible might take a picture of a shy octopus with long **tentacles**, or even discover a new underwater species that has never been seen before. It might capture images of fish that use chemicals in their bodies to give off light and live in the deepest parts of the sea, in regions too far below the surface for sunlight to reach. Thanks to ROVs, these strange fish and other animals are no longer hidden from us.

13

Without a little submersible named *Alvin*, scientists may never have found the *Titanic*.

ALVIN

Alvin and the Titanic

One of the most famous submersibles is a little vehicle named *Alvin*. This submersible has been exploring the deep sea for decades. In 1986 *Alvin* was used by scientist Robert Ballard to find and explore the shipwrecked ocean liner, the RMS *Titanic*. The *Titanic* hit an iceberg and sank to the bottom of the ocean in 1912. The wreckage had never been located.

But thanks to the help of *Alvin* and an ROV named *J.J.*, the exploration of *Titanic* was possible in the North Atlantic Ocean, nearly seventy-five years after it sank! The wreck was found in pieces, in areas as deep as 12,500 feet below the surface. More than 60,000 pictures and over sixty hours of video were taken as every inch of the *Titanic* was explored. For the first time, people were able to see the wreckage of the world's most famous ship.

Submersibles helped figure out
how the *Titanic* sank.

Alvin and *J.J.* did more than just photograph an old
shipwreck. After scientists studied the images, they
discovered that the most famous theory about how
the ship sank was not possible. Up until then, scientists
believed that the iceberg the ship had hit created a 300-
foot gash in the side of the ship, which caused it to sink.
But the photos from the submersible revealed that this
gash does not exist. Instead, the photos showed that
the ship might have sunk after it had split in the middle,
causing water to flood into the boat.

The discovery of the *Titanic* was reported all over the
world, and submersibles were able to recover priceless
treasures that were aboard the luxury liner.

Since *Alvin* made its first dive in 1964, it has made more than four thousand trips to the ocean depths. It has discovered giant tubeworms and repaired pipelines on the ocean floor. Once it was attacked by a swordfish, which was hauled back to the surface and cooked for dinner!

In the Control Room

Some of the most highly trained oceanographers in the world operate submersibles on their underwater missions. Some do so while sitting inside the submersible,

Scientists can control Remotely Operated Vehicle submersibles from miles away.

while others operate the vehicle by remote control from miles away.

Before any submersible is launched from a ship, the ship's captain must decide whether the weather is good enough for the journey. Water that is too rough can force the submersible off course.

The launching ship's crew must also plan ahead for the amount of time the submersible will be underwater so that passengers will have enough oxygen for their trip. If the submersible crew plans to collect samples of ocean life, they must include the correct sampling containers when equipping the vessel.

Jacques Cousteau became the face of undersea exploration after helping to invent the Aqualung.

In 1960 Jacques Piccard and Don Walsh piloted *Trieste* nearly seven miles under the ocean's surface.

Famous Underwater Explorers

One of the most famous underwater explorers, even to this day, is Jacques Cousteau. In 1943 he invented the Aqualung, a device that provides divers with oxygen from a tank they wear on their backs. For the first time, divers could stay under water for ninety minutes or more. This excited many explorers with the possibility of reaching new depths of the ocean. Besides making contributions to underwater technology, Cousteau also made TV shows and films about the ocean that helped the public learn more about this unexplored area of our Earth.

In 1960 two other famous oceanographers, Jacques Piccard and Don Walsh, piloted a bathyscaphe named *Trieste* to record-breaking depths of nearly seven miles in the Mariana Trench of the western Pacific. Their record has remained unbroken for almost fifty years.

Sylvia Earle once lived in an underwater laboratory for two weeks.

Robert Ballard discovered the *Titanic's* wreckage with the help of submersibles.

Some ocean explorers have focused more on biological discoveries than on breaking records. Sylvia Earle is a marine biologist who has a special interest in ocean life in the deep sea. She has discovered many new species of marine life and has even lived in an underwater laboratory for two weeks with a crew of explorers. She has also made people aware of the problems our oceans face as a result of pollution caused by humans.

Robert Ballard has changed the way underwater explorers work by using submersibles and ROVs. His discovery of the *Titanic* wreckage and other shipwrecks has made him one of the world's most highly respected scientists in underwater research.

Each new explorer solves a few more mysteries of the ocean. Despite amazing discoveries, an ocean researcher might work tirelessly without a boost to his or her **ego**. They explore, experiment, and engineer, because they love the ocean.

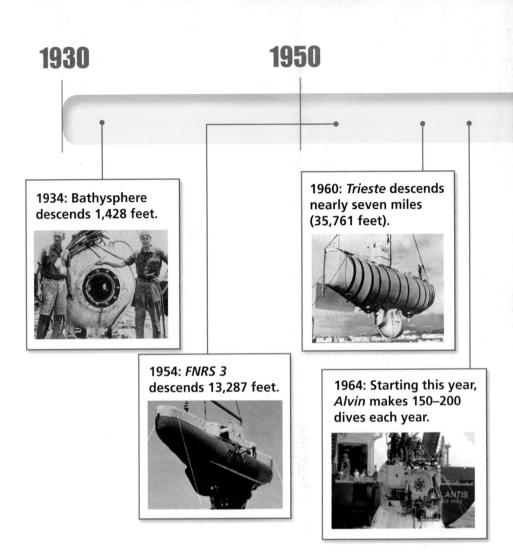

1930

1950

1934: Bathysphere descends 1,428 feet.

1960: *Trieste* descends nearly seven miles (35,761 feet).

1954: *FNRS 3* descends 13,287 feet.

1964: Starting this year, *Alvin* makes 150–200 dives each year.

Researching Deeper with Time

Since submersibles were invented, they have improved and reached new depths. They have explored new worlds and collected amazing corals, animals, and other sea life. With each new invention or robotic device, submersibles become more useful to scientists and more powerful tools in helping scientists discover more about the mysteries of the deep ocean. From the bathysphere in 1930 to the models being invented today, submersibles are doing the jobs that scientists wish they could do themselves.

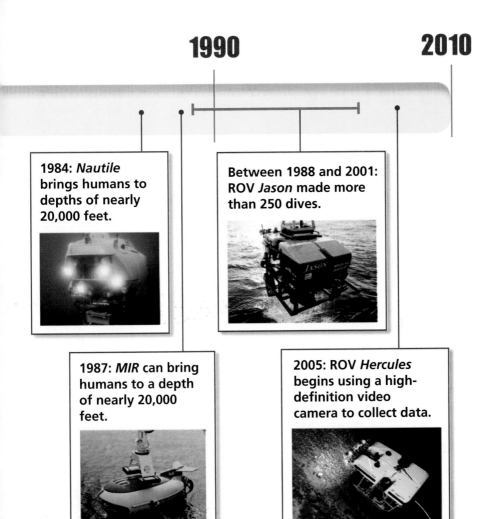

1990

2010

1984: *Nautile* brings humans to depths of nearly 20,000 feet.

Between 1988 and 2001: ROV *Jason* made more than 250 dives.

1987: *MIR* can bring humans to a depth of nearly 20,000 feet.

2005: ROV *Hercules* begins using a high-definition video camera to collect data.

Submersibles reach into an underwater world, often to places people cannot go. When they explore these deep places far beneath the ocean's surface, they collect useful and valuable research data for scientists to study. Not only can they help discover new species of sea animals, but they can also capture data about animal behavior, survival methods, and ecosystems. For example, researchers can compare their observations about where they have or have not seen a particular kind of animal. This gives scientists valuable information about the population range and habitat of the animal.

Into the Future

Scientists believe we have a duty to preserve the ocean habitats as we discover more about them. Our growing knowledge of the ocean can help us learn more about life on land. But without the submersibles, many of our newest ocean discoveries would probably not have been made. These small vehicles that explore greater and greater depths have extended the reach of our own eyes and ears.

We can only guess what the future of ocean exploration will bring. Submersible technology will help answer more questions about the ocean and its living things. Whatever we find is also likely to raise more questions—and a new awareness of our oceans' worth.

What will submersibles find in the future?

Glossary

ego *n.* conceit, self-importance; a person's self-worth.

hatch *n.* a small opening for a person to fit through.

intrepid *adj.* fearless or adventurous.

propulsion *n.* the means by which something is moved forward.

silt *n.* a fine sand or clay that is carried by running water and deposited.

submersible *n.* a small submarine-like vehicle for underwater exploration.

tentacles *n.* thin limbs on an animal such as an octopus.

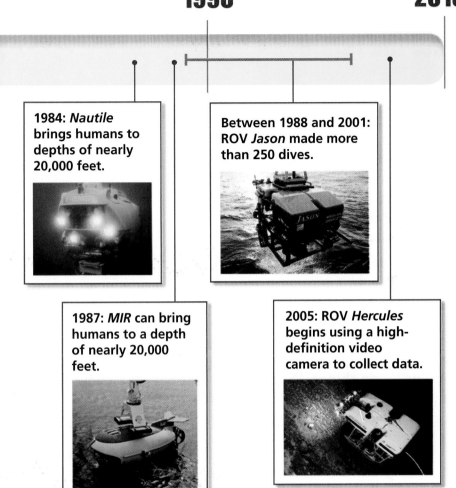

Photographs

ISBN 13: 978-0-328-52622-2
ISBN 10:   0-328-52622-3

3 4 5 6 7 V0N4 17 16 15 14 13 12 11 10

A. Engine-Room.—C. Smoke-Stack.—D. Munition-Room.—E. Coal-Bunkers.—F. Look-Out.—I. I, I. Compartments for Air or Water.—6, 6, 6. Compartments for Compressed Air

LONGITUDINAL SECTION OF SUBMARINE BATTERY.

How Low Can You Go?

In the 1600s, the first true submarine was invented. It carried a crew of people and traveled under the ocean's surface as well as floating on top of it. Over the years and centuries that followed, subs became reliable enough for both transportation and warfare. Today's submarines can be as small as a car or as large as two jumbo-jets. Some submarines are designed for short trips, while others can go around the world without refueling. But they are rarely used for exploring the ocean bottom.

Ocean explorers wanted a device that could go into the deeper parts of the ocean, far from shore. For many years, most submarines went only a few hundred feet below the surface of the ocean. This is because the water pressure at lower depths is greater than the submarines could bear.

The weight of water puts pressure on any object in the ocean. The deeper an object is in the ocean, the more water pressure the object has to withstand. Going

Photographs

Every effort has been made to secure permission and provide appropriate credit for photographic material. The publisher deeply regrets any omission and pledges to correct errors called to its attention in subsequent editions.

Unless otherwise acknowledged, all photographs are the property of Pearson Education, Inc.

Photo locators denoted as follows: Top (T), Center (C), Bottom (B), Left (L), Right (R), Background (Bkgd)

ISBN 13: 978-0-328-52622-2
ISBN 10:   0-328-52622-3

3 4 5 6 7 V0N4 17 16 15 14 13 12 11 10

What will
submersibles find
in the future?

23